My ADHD Story

By A and A North

Published by Rio Way Press
Written and illustrated by A and A North

First edition 2026

ISBN: 978-1-7646742-0-1

This book is dedicated to
all the children who feel like they are "too
much."
Too loud, too quiet, too busy, too
sensitive,
or just a little bit different.

You are not too much.
You are exactly enough.

Hi, It's nice to meet you!
My name is:

____

I have ADHD

(Attention Deficit Hyperactivity Disorder.)

MY EMOTIONS WHEEL

How are you feeling today?

Sometimes it's hard for me to explain what's happening in my brain or how i'm feeling.

That's why I'm sharing this book.
This is my voice on the page, telling
you my ADHD story.

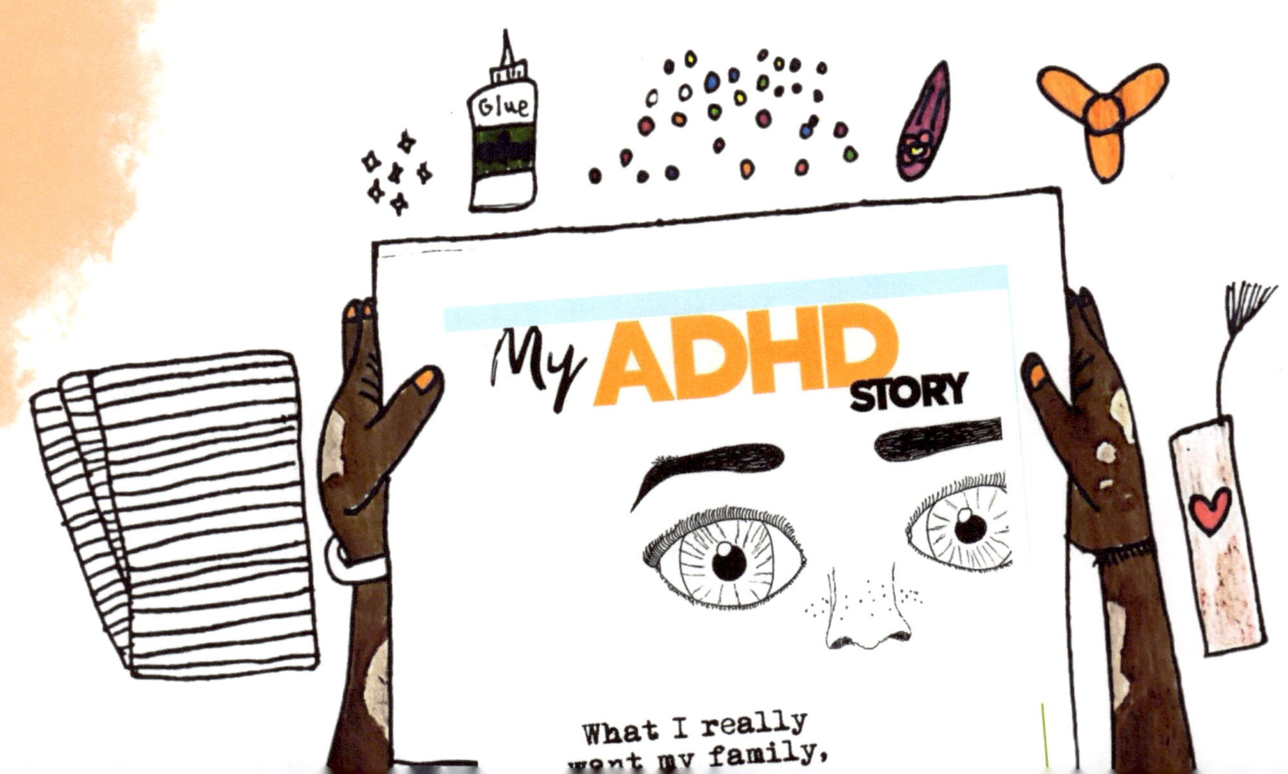

This is my way of advocating
for myself.

It's my way of saying

"Here's who I am, and here's how
you can help me shine!"

Now I'm going to show you
what it feels like for me.

Love from,

Let me explain ADHD

Having ADHD means my brain works a bit differently
to some other kids' brains.

My brain has lots of thoughts, ideas and feelings all at
once. Thoughts can pop into my brain really fast. Like
popcorn!

This can make school and listening feel hard.

But it also makes me creative,
curious and full of imagination.

What ADHD Means to Me

Everyone's ADHD looks a little different.
This is what it feels like for me:

My brain can be fast — zooming with ideas, thoughts, and questions.

My brain is full of creativity and imagination. It can't switch off! This is called "hyperfocus".

My brain can be busy noticing absolutely everything around me. I try my best to listen, but sometimes it feels impossible.

I can feel really tired,
just trying to keep up.
You might notice I yawn a lot.

I can feel full of worries and
anxiety. Sometimes I freeze
and need a little time before I
can talk.

ADHD isn't something "wrong."

It's just a different kind of brain magic.
And I want you to understand my kind.

To me, ADHD feels like...

This is your page.
Draw what ADHD feels like for you.

Sometimes my brain can feel like a bouncy ball.
Sometimes it feels like a superhero.
And sometimes it feels tired or overwhelmed
and that's okay too.

This is MY brain,

and I'm learning more about it every day.

When Words Get Stuck Inside Me

Some days, I want to tell my teacher what I need...
but the words hide.

They sit behind my lips like shy little turtles.
I know what I want to say,
but it feels scary to speak up.
That's when I remind myself:

I'm allowed to ask for help.

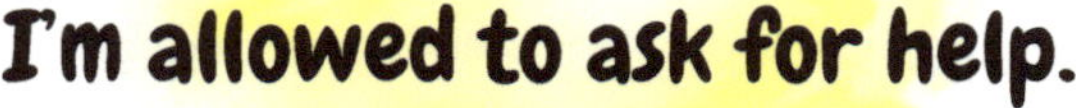

I don't have to be brave all at once.
Asking for help is practising bravery.

My Helper Words

When it's too hard to say everything,
I use my helper words.
These are little sentences that make big things easier:

"I need a break, please."
"Can you explain that again?"
"Can I move while I listen?"
"I'm trying my best."

Helper words are like keys.
They open doors so adults know how to support me.

When I'm finding schoolwork hard

It might look like I'm not trying, but inside, I don't know where to start.

Sometimes my brain gets stuck.

When this happens, I need a little help to get going again.

You Can Help Me By

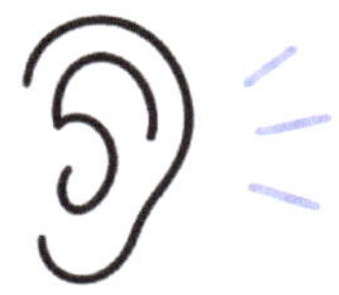

- Staying calm when I feel overwhelmed

- Noticing when I'm trying

- Giving me time to think

- Helping me restart instead of giving up

- Reminding me that mistakes are okay

Things That Help Me Learn

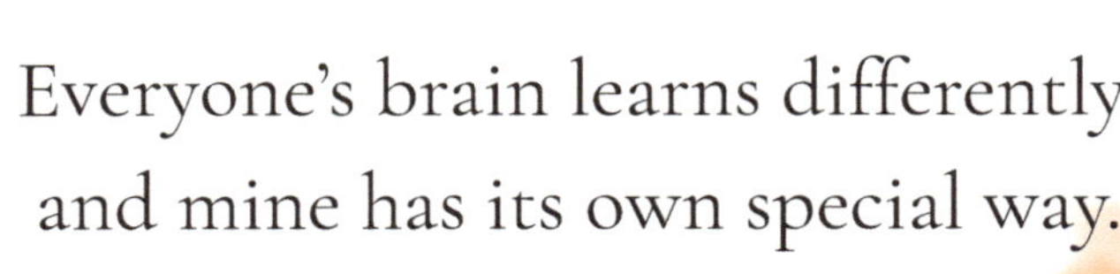

Everyone's brain learns differently,
and mine has its own special way.

These are the things that help my brain do its best:

**Taking small breaks when my mind
feels too full.**

**Moving my body—a wiggle, a
stretch, or tapping my feet.**

**Using fidgets so my hands can stay
busy while I listen.**

**Clear steps that show me what to
do first, next, and last.**

Pictures or colour coding help me remember.

Extra time helps me not feel rushed.

Quiet corners help when my brain needs calm to concentrate.

Extra reminders help me stay on track.

When I use the tools that help me learn,
I feel proud, capable, and ready to shine.

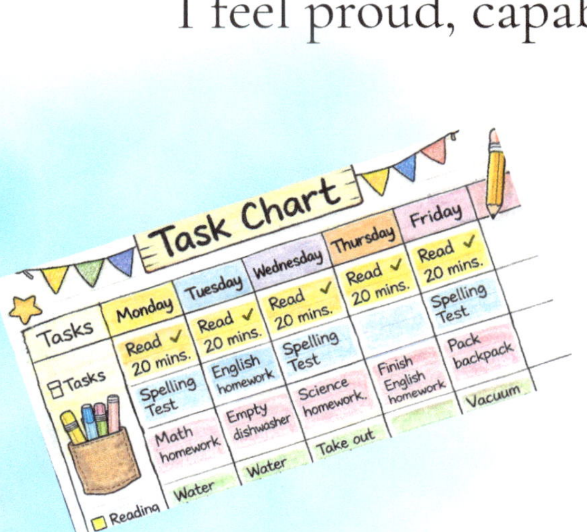

When I feel upset at school

Sometimes I feel really upset at school and I don't always know why.
This might look like me being quiet, teary, angry, or wanting to be alone.

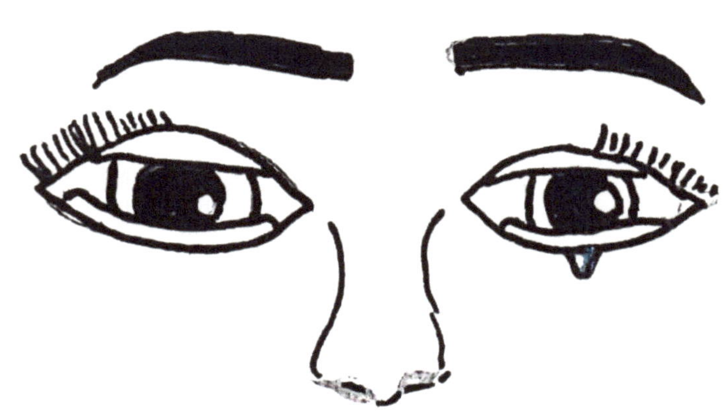

My brain can feel overwhelmed.
It really helps me when I can take a short break,
go to a calm space, or be with someone who understands.

When My Body Wants to Move

My legs wiggle.
My fingers tap.

My tummy feels full of butterflies.
My body tries to remind me that

moving helps me think.

And that's not bad, it's just how my body works.
Sometimes I need to stretch, walk, rock, or fidget.

Movement is not misbehaving.
Movement is a need.

My Super Strengths

ADHD isn't just about challenges. It's full of strengths. These are my powers.

Ideas Power –
I think of ideas quickly.

Creative Power –
My imagination is big and full of creativity.

Heart Power –
I care deeply about people and the world around me.

Focus Power –
When I love something, I can focus for a long time.

Energy Power –
I bring excitement to everything I do.

My Support Crew

I'm not alone.

I have a whole team helping me shine —
my teacher, my parents, my friends...
and me.

When I need help, I can :

- **Write it**
- **Point to it**
- **Show a card**
- **Say it out loud**

If my words come out too fast,
I can try again. If I feel quiet, I might need time.

Every part of me is okay.

My support crew understands me.

What My Support Crew Wants You To Know

I am great at:

I thrive when:

Things I Want You to Know About Me

There are a few things I really want people to understand.
These things help me feel safe, supported, and seen.

I am great at:

The people who love me say I am:

One thing that makes me special is...

You might see me **moving** around, **talking** fast,
having big
feelings, or getting **excited**.

They are all part of who I am.

Thank you for taking the time to learn about
my ADHD
and what helps me thrive.

Let's work together
so I can feel understood
and do my best.

How to Use This Book

This book is here to help children share who they are, in their own way.

Some children may like to read it from start to finish.
Others may choose to flick to the pages that feel important to them.

You can:
- Add your own thoughts
- Cross out parts that don't feel right
- Share pages with teachers, family, or friends
- Come back to it whenever you need

**There is no right or wrong way to use this book.
It belongs to you.**

Coming Soon

My ADHD STORY
and friendships
Written and Illustrated
by A and A North

My ADHD STORY
and school
SCHOOL
Written and Illustrated by
A and A North

Y.N.T.M.
YOU'RE NOT TOO MUCH

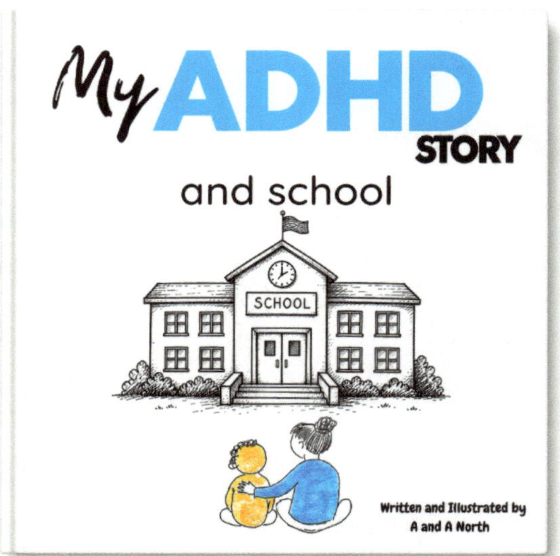

www.ingramcontent.com/pod-product-compliance
Lightning Source LLC
Chambersburg PA
CBHW042132030726
47599CB00002B/441